Google Classroom:

2018 User Manual to Learn Everything You Need to Know About Google Classroom

ISBN: 1726455416
ISBN-13: 978-1726455411

CONTENTS

Thank you for purchasing this book!

We always try to give more value then you expect. That's why we've updated the content and you can get it for FREE. You can get the digital version for free because you bought the print version.

The book is under the match program from Amazon. You can find how to do this using next URL: https://www.amazon.com/gp/digital/ep-landing-page

I hope it will be useful for you.

Introduction

Do you know about Google Classroom?

Google Classroom is essentially Google's answer to helping you plan your semesters as a teacher. It's a helpful platform, used by teachers and students alike, and it can change the way classes are ran.

But, do you know how to use it? This system does involve plan books and different activities that are put together in order to help a student better understand the curriculum, and it might be a bit overwhelming for a few people.

Fortunately, though, it's very easy to use, and luckily quite user-friendly. You can always go to G-suite for any questions as a teacher, but this book will tell you everything that you need to know about Google Classroom, including various aspects of this that are a bit different from other platforms. This is a virtual platform that can change your life, and one that allows you to easily plan your semester, and all of the lessons that you want to plan easily, and without too much effort.

But, you may log into the system and then be totally confused. That's okay. This book will go over each step, and from there, you'll be able to take this into your own hands. The best part, is that you can pair this with other interactive software devices as well, and from there, create the perfect environment for yourself, and for your classroom, so you'll be able to easily create the perfect lesson plan, and an easy semester to run.

Not only that, it keeps getting new updates constantly, so you'll be able to have a more streamlined experience with this software. So what are you waiting for? If you're ready to take your classroom to the technology age, then this I the way to go, and this is something that will make your life even easier than ever before. It's certainly a different style of teaching and learning, but it's not a bad one, that's for sure.

1 Chapter – Benefits of Google Classroom for Everyone!

For many educators, they may see that it's a great system, but who else can benefit from this? Well, let's talk about how it benefits everyone, including teachers, students, and parents. This chapter will tell you all about the benefits of Google Classroom for everyone, and why it matters.

Less Paperwork!

This is a benefit for everyone. Do you as a teacher tend to have worksheets that students may come to you days later to tell you that they lost it? Or maybe you need a new roll book for attendance? Or maybe you have this worksheet that you've found, but don't want to waste valuable class time trying to copy it? Or maybe you just don't want to deal with papers upon papers? If you're sick of it, then Google Classroom is for you. With this system, you can create worksheets in the Google drive, share it to the class, or even make a form for students to fill out. You can use the "share to classroom" feature in order to share new and valuable items to the classroom. Not only that, you can create a digital logbook which in turn will save you lots of paper. If you want to save yourself stress, and save the environment as well, then Google Classroom is the way to go, because it uses so much less energy. Everyone can be on the same page, and creates a collaboration not seen before.

Managing Workflow

If you have assignments that involve having them all collected at once, then you should start using Google Classroom. This actually can tell you in real-time the progress of a student to see who's done and not done, allowing you to see the status of students who are missing items, and you can timestamp everything, so you won't allow late work to slide. For teachers as well, you can actually go to the screen that says student work, and see the progress on there, since it's actually all tied into Google docs or slides. It allows you to see any revisions that you see as well, and you can see the student production too. That way, everyone is watched, and you can help with the student's progress as needed.

Allows the use of Online Learning Platforms

One nice thing about Google Classroom is that it's so easy. For many students, when they get to college, they may be confused by the idea of degree work online. However, online classes are super popular, so if you want to get them ahead of the game, you should expose them to what it's like to have an online-only education. Google classroom is a great way to do this, because it's super easy for everyone, and most students love it, since everything is there.

Better engagement

With Google Classroom, it brings forth more engagement because of one aspect people both laud and chide: technology. Technology is one of the biggest benefits to using Google Classroom. Children use technology almost all the time now, from browsing social media to using the internet for research. Why not make everything infused with technology? Whether you're for it or not, if you want to get students to answer questions and develop understanding, then this is the way to go. It'll allow you to build better interest in every student as well.

Gets better Conversations going

Sometimes, it's very awkward trying to ask questions, and students are either too nervous to speak, or maybe they don't want to, or they often are stunted on deepening though. But, did you know that you could get more engagement from students in a better way through the use of Google Classroom. Just posting a question in the questions area will get students to comment. The best part, is other students can comment there, and it can deepen the way students do learn the coursework, and it can make your life easier. Even the most socially awkward of students will benefit from this, because it's easier to say things online than in person, and it can make a world of a difference in the long run.

Easy Support

One thing that's great about this, is that if you're a teacher or an administrator, and don't know how to use this, you can get the help that you need. With G suite, you'll be able to use Google Classroom easily with their helpful how-to software, set permissions, have some support at all times of the day, and you actually can use this software and protect the data and classes. It's a secure software that really will help you, and ultimately will really make your classroom easier to manage. The support can be directly with another person, or you can view some of the tutorials that you may be interested in if you're looking to get better with this site and interface, this is ultimately the way to go. You can use a lot of different help tools in order to really benefit from this.

Can't Lose Work Anymore

If you're a teacher, chances are you've had to deal with the lost work excuses. Students lose work when it's on paper, or it involves a physical object. But, did you know that with this system, it actually eliminates the chances of you losing it. Since Google classroom eliminates the consumption of paper, so long as you've got access to the internet, you'll be okay, and ultimately, it actually will save your district a ton of money on paper. It's quite nice, and it does the job.

Along with that, since it is cloud-based, no matter what computer you're on, you'll be able to access your work. If you have everything on a cloud, it's based off an internet connection rather than a hard drive. You may have heard the excuse from a student that they had a hard drive failure, which is why they couldn't save it or turn it in. but with Google Classroom, it actually can be accessed through all devices, and students can work wherever they are, not have to worry about a flash drive not reading or losing your work, and it eliminates the uses of emails constantly. Plus, all of this saves to the drive immediately, so if there is a computer hiccup, you don't have to worry about losing progress or anything. You don't have to hear the excuse that the computer crashed, or you left the flash drive at home, since you're essentially going to be able to access everything through the internet.

Apps Galore

Google Classroom functions well on a mobile device, which means that you can take this on the go as well. Lots of times, students will make the excuse of they weren't on the computer or saw the assignment, but if they have a phone, you download the app, and you get announcements and various assignments that are posted, so you can stay on top of these. Teachers as well can post in real time any of the assignments that they need, through the app or the sharing support with this, and it's super convenient, and makes your life as a teacher that much easier.

Ease of Workflow

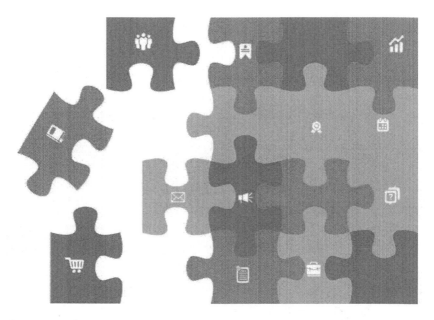

The nice thing about this, is that with the interface, you can add on some products that sync over with Google Classroom, and you can put extra add-ons and apps within this so that you've got a full-on classroom environment. You can track the trends, users, and even students, and administrators of the Google Classroom platform will give students and teachers a better platform over time. Plus, this is always updating, so you'll have the support that you want to.

Real time feedback

One thing that's super nice about this platform, is the fact that teachers can give feedback right away. With each assignment uploaded, the teacher can go through, make some notes, and then give the students feedback that they want. They can reach out immediately if the student is struggling and work with them as needed.

Can Upload Resources

if you have students that need extra copies, you as a teacher don't need to worry about that. What you do, is upload the forms for assignments straight into Google Classroom, and from there, the students can take control over this. If a student misses an assignment, tell them it's in Google Classroom, and from there, you can have students check that whenever possible. It's quite simple.

Saves you SO Much money

One thing that is really nice about this, is the price of Google Classroom. It's free. It saves you a ton of money since everything is paperless and on a drive. You can install free apps on this to really help you get the most out of this, and you'll be able to easily, and without fail, create the lesson plans that you want, and the classroom you desire. It's quite nice, and you can differentiate all of these between classes too. Plus, with constant improvements, it's always growing.

Google Classroom is the future, and you'll be able to easily and without fail really make it better for every student. You don't have to worry about students falling behind, but instead, you'll be able to create a better learning environment that will make everything better.

2 Chapter — Getting Started with Google Classroom

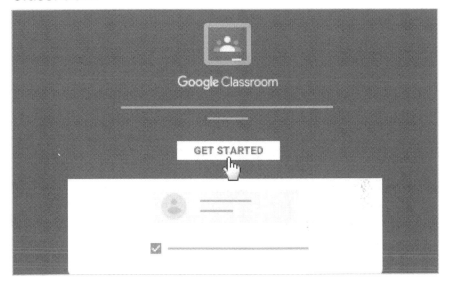

Now, Google classroom has lots of benefits to it. We will tell you what you can get out of this as a teacher, and how you can start with creating plans on this. If you're ready to explore Google classroom, then this chapter is good for you.

What Teachers and Students can Do with This?

What teachers can do with this is actually quite awesome. If you've ever wanted to manage a class directly without any problems, or even just ditching the paperwork, then this is the way to go.

In this, you can do the following, but of course it's not just limited to this:

- Create classes

- Manage classes

- Put together some amazing assignments, even using extensions

- Grade everything right in one place

- Give feedback on everything that you provide to students

- Help those as needed

- Add some extra learning extensions to help with improving your understanding of this system.

For students, you can do virtually the same thing that teachers can do, but on the student end:

- Get your grades from the teacher

- Get help on a subject as needed

- Turn in assignments, which essentially helps ditch the paper and minimizes excuses

- Talk to other students through the stream or email, which helps out a lot if you're struggling with classes

- Keep track of all of the materials and coursework all in one place

This is awesome software for students because it puts everything all in one place, and it does help students with keeping everything in order

How to Get Started

Now you know what this does for teachers and students, but

how do you get started? Well, what you need t do, is first make sure that you have an existing Google account. If that's not already done, then you'll need to make that. It's quite simple, and it's really just your email and password. Then, you want to choose the option to go to classroom.Google.com account. For teachers, once you do this, you'll sign in, and then you'll get a handy welcome screen. From there, you'll then be able to create a class, and we will discuss how you create, manage them, and even how to remove them in the next section.

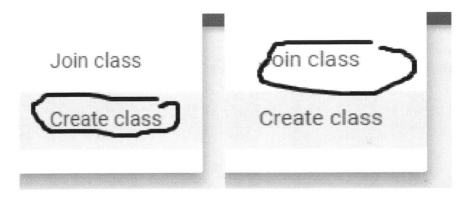

By understanding how to use this, and the importance of this for teachers, and how you essentially get started, you'll be well on your way to using Google Classroom with everything, and it'll make everything all the more easier.

3 Chapter – How to Create and Manage a Class

Classes are fun to create, and we will go over in this chapter how you create a class, organize and manage the class, and how you can remove classes once they are done. Classes are the most important aspect of this, since it's where everyone will be, and if you know how to put all of this together, you'll be well on your way to a successful result with Google Classroom.

How to create a Class

now, once you've logged in and everything, it's time to create a class. When you first do log in, you get the option of either student, or teacher. Always make sure that you indicate that you are a teacher, and if you mess up, you need to contact the administrator to reset this. It's super important, because students are limited in their options compared to teachers, and it can be quite frustrating. Now, if you're a student, you simply press when you get the plus button to join a class. For teachers, it's create a class.

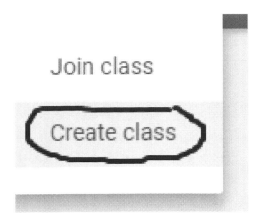

Now, if you've already got classes, chances are you'll see some other names there. They'll be displayed on the screen itself, but every time you press the plus button, you'll then be able to add more to this.

Next, you're given a class dialogue boss. you'll then type in the name, and the section of this. you'll be able to immediately create the class from here.

But, if you want to add more to it, you can go to the about tab, choose the title of the course, along with the description of this, the location of this, and even add materials here. You do need to have a name for the class itself, since this is how students will find the class when they open it up. If you have classes with multiple names on it, you'll definitely want to specify, either via time or day, especially if you've got a lot of sections. The section field is how you do this, and you can create a subject as well, based on the list of subjects they provide for you.

Some teachers like to make these very descriptive, and you should ideally add as much information as you feel that you need for this. But do remember, that you make sure that it isn't some wall of text that students will read and get confused. As a teacher, you should make sure that you do this in a way where students will get the information easily, and that they'll be able to delineate each class. It's also important to make it easy for your own benefit.

Class settings

x

Class 1223

A subject on ___

Room 2238

CANCEL   SAVE

How to manage a Class

First thing that you can do when changing the class and managing it, is giving it a theme. One thing that you'll notice is that you don't have students in there once it's created, so you can have a bit of fun with this. One way you can do it, is on the right side near the header of the general class, is you need to change the class theme. You can use the themes that are there to be offered. Some photos of classes themselves are good options, and you can use different templates for each one so that you know exactly what class you're using, because themes can sometimes be a bit complicated.

Gallery   x

Gallery   Patterns

Select Class Theme   Cancel

How to Remove, Delete, and View a Class

When using Google Classroom, sometimes you'll want to delete a class when it's the end of the semester, and you can always restore it as needed if you need it. You can also delete it if you never want to see the class again, or have no use for it because you've got the assignments already. Now, if you don't achieve these, they stick around, so make sure that you achieve them.

Now archived classes essentially means that they're in an area where you have the materials, the work students have, and the posts. You can view it, but you can't actually use it, and is good if a student wants the materials.

Archiving classes is simple to do. You choose the class, see the three dots, press, it and then, it's archived.

Now to view an archived class after it's been archived, you press the three line menu, go down to the tab that says achieve classes, and then choose the class you want to see.

To delete a class though, you essentially want to do the same thing. Remember, that you need to achieve the class before you can delete it, so scroll all the way down, choose achieve classes, and from there, once you have the classes, you want to press the three dots option, and then choose to delete this. From there, you'll have the class fully removed. Remember though, you can't undo this once you've done this, and if you do choose to delete a class, you don't have access to the comments or the posts, but if you have any files that are in the drive, you can always access those, since you have those in the class files themselves.

Other Tips and Tricks for class Management

There are a few class management things that you can implement, and some tips and tricks that go into Google Classroom. The first thing that happens, is that when you get to the classes tab on there, and you want to drag and move the classes around, you could do so. This is a good way to change the order of this, and it's quite easy to do.

Another important thing to remember too, is that you have the classroom function. It's quite nice, and if you want to change the calendar or view it, you essentially can press the icon with the calendar that's on there, and you can even check it out to see what's coming up for every single class, because some classes may do certain things at different times of the semester.

Finally, you can always adjust the settings at any point. This is done with the gear that you see on the home screen. Here, you can change the name of the class, especially if it's confusing, show the class code if you need it, and also decide on the stream and also to showcase whether or not you want items to be deleted or displayed. There are other features there too, and it's all right there waiting for you to be used.

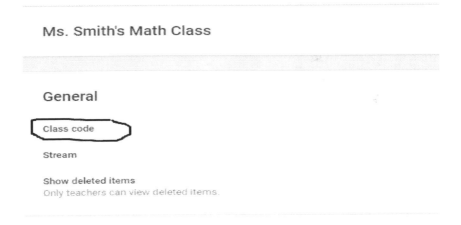

Ms. Smith's Math Class

General

Class code

Stream

Show deleted items
Only teachers can view deleted items.

When it comes to Google Classroom, knowing how to create the classes is a big part of it. If you have classes that you want to add, or you want to get started with Google Classroom, this is the way to go, and it's the surefire way to success with this.

4 Chapter – How to Set Due Dates, Manage homework, and Assignments

Obviously a big part of teaching is well, assignments and homework. Managing all of this is a big part of teaching, and this chapter will go over everything that you need to know about managing this, including streams, announcements, homework, assignments, and how you can manage it all easily.

The Stream

First thing we will discuss is the stream. This is essentially how communication is managed at this point. If you're familiar with social media, this is essentially like Facebook, and it's how members of each class communicate, and both teachers and students use this. Of course, if you have a class that has questions, you can essentially just respond to the question as it's asked.

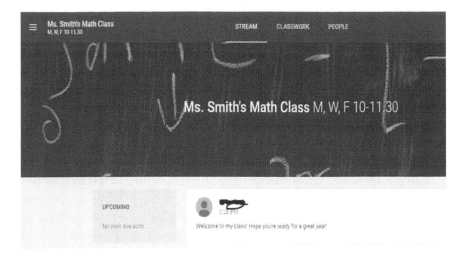

To begin with this, once you have a class made, you press the plus button, and from there, choose the option to create a post. If you don't see it highlighted, that means that someone turned off posts. You can write the comment, and then post it. You can from there, add attachments through pressing the paperclip that you see there, and then you can add that as an attachment to the stream.

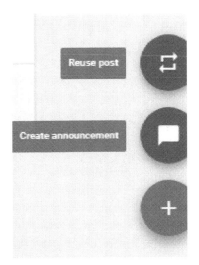

You also have other options too. You can create an announcement, an assignment, a question, or even reusing posts whenever possible. Just choose the option, and then, you can then post it. Sometimes, attaching a topic to this is another great option too.

Scheduling and reusing posts

Scheduling and reusing posts are something teachers do, especially if they have an assignment that they liked. To schedule a post, you can create it so that it appears at a time and date. To do this, you press the option to create a post or assignment, and then on the side, you'll see a tab that has a plus sign on it. Press that, and you'll then be given the option to schedule this. From there, you can put in when it should appear on the stream, and then it'll happen. You can then finish up, and there you go. This is great for teachers that don't want to have to spend copious amounts of time scheduling.

Emailing students

Some teachers like to email students instead of just commenting on streams and such. If that's the case, you can go to the students tab. Usually, they see the names, and you can choose the student, or students to email, and then, you'll see three dots, which from there gives you the action to email students. Students can email the teacher by going to the three dots next to the name of the teacher, and from there, Gmail will open automatically, and the teacher's email address will be in there. They can also go to the students' tab, choose the student to email, and then go to the three dots and choose to email the student. This is no ideal way to communicate, but it's a way to do so.

Announcements

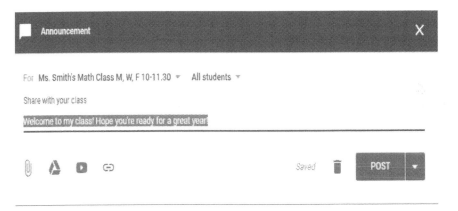

Announcements are great ways to communicate general information to the class, whether it be saying hello, making sure to remind them, or even giving them some information on something to help them better understand a project or subject in class. To do this, you want to press the plus sign on the right corner, and when you're given options, choose the option to create an announcement. You can from there, attach files using the paperclip option once again, or even use various links to sources that you've found. It's quite nice, and it certainly does the job.

Lots of teachers like the announcement system, and students can comment on there to any announcement that they see, unless you've turned it off, and students can also use it to communicate with you. If you're just now getting used to using this, you should use this as an introductory device. You can put a welcome announcement, have the students comment, or just write how you're excited to be their teacher this year. You can also tell students that commenting is super helpful for this, and that they should be able to easily use this, and learn how to master this system.

Making Assignments in Google Classroom

Making assignments and homework is a huge part of a teacher's job. Did you know that they are pretty simple to make though? The first thing that you'll want to do, is when you title these, always make sure that you do have a number on these, such as 001 if you're going to have over 100 assignments for the class. This is super important, since it makes it easier for students to find the assignment in Google Classroom, and it's good since it'll give you a chance to create an order in case if you accidentally assign something out of order.

Now to begin, you want to go to the class that gets the assignment, and from there, you will want to go to the plus sign that you see, and you're given the option to create assignment.

Now with this, you'll see immediately that you're given a header. you'll want to make sure that you do think carefully about this, since as soon as you assign it, you'll see a folder created for it, and the title of this does match the header of this, so definitely be mindful of mistakes.

Now from here, you essentially give a description of the assignment, and make sure that this is long enough for the student to go back to later, or if they missed it.

You can also choose the due date for this. You essentially choose the date it's due, and it also gives you the time option, if you want it by a time on a date.

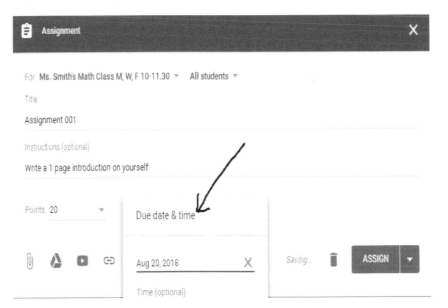

Now another big part of this is points. Lots of classes do the point system, and it's a huge part of many curriculum, and this can be changed. You can assign point value to this by adding in manually how many points you want to add to this, or if you want it to be ungraded, you can use the drop-down menu to change this.

Finally, you've got the chance to add attachments. You can create templates in Google drive, and then add them to here, and the student can then fill them out. You can also give links to students too if you want them to use a link to fill out the assignment that they have.

If you do want to assign this to multiple classes, you choose the class near the top, and then all of the classes to assign the work to.

Assignments in Google Drive

When choosing to use Google Classroom, sometimes the teachers create assignments from the drive. For example, maybe there's a worksheet that can be used that they scan and put on the drive itself. This is actually how the resources are kept for teachers. Now, when you have an assignment that you want to put on there, you essentially need to go to the Google drive, and make sure that you choose the right option. That's because you get three different choices, and they are as follows:

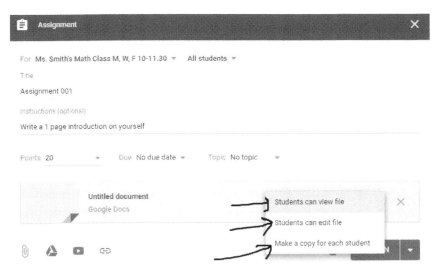

Within these options, you get the following, and these appear every time you put a Google document on there:

- Students can view the file: basically means they can look for it, but aren't allowed to modify, as in the case of study guides and handouts

- Students can edit the file: this is where they can edit the document and then work on it, which works for collaborative projects that students do together, such as various projects that they do, including group projects. Slides for an assignments are good for this too, or where they put together brainstorming ideas

- Make a copy: this is a way where you can choose to make a copy of the file to every single student, and they get individual editing rights for this. The master is intact, and students can't access it, but they get to fill out the other one, and this is good for any assignments that involve filling out questions, or worksheets and such.

This is a good option if you're wondering whether or not you should assign it to a few, or to many.

Student Assignment Views

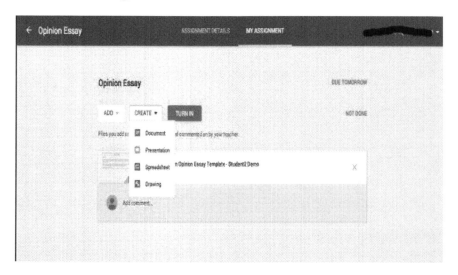

For students, it's a bit different, since they will see a different view compared to teachers. Essentially, they see the description for the assignment, and in it, you see a button that says open, and from there, the student will put the assignment into there. you'll want to make sure that you inform the students that they need to choose whether they are marking it as done or turning it in, depending on if they have to turn in anything or if they don't.

How Students Interact with the Assignment

Now for students, when they choose to turn in an assignment, there are two things to realize. If you see a form with them, choose the form and answer the questions that you have, and then submit, mark it as done, and then make sure to confirm it. you'll then see that the assignment is marked as done. If you see more, you should go to open assignment, and then fill out the rest.

With a document, it's similar in a sense. You basically do the job, turn it in, and then, you'll see that when it's turned in, it'll be labeled with the name.

For attaching, you go to add on the assignment, click on the arrow, and then choose to attach a file via either drive, or a file itself. You then can attach, and turn it in.

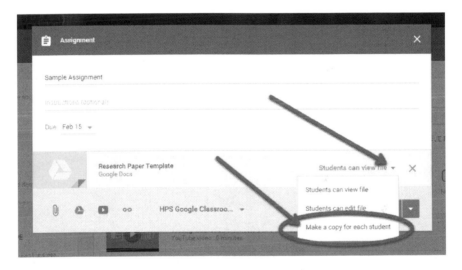

For assignments that don't involve actually turning in anything, or maybe you want to comment on something, you touch the assignment, add the comment if needed, and then choose to mark it as done. If you have an assignment you want to change, choose it, and then press unsubmit, and then there you go.

For teachers, you want to go to the pop-up menu, and it shows the assignments, and which ones will be overdue, and you can even see the grades that are there. It's a good way to see it, and students can also check this if they want to submit assignments.

Organizing class Topics

With a class, you usually have different units, chapters, and the like. It can be a bit overwhelming if you don't have a decent system for this. You can however, use topics to make it easier.

To do this, you want to go to classwork, and then under the section, you press the create button, and then you can choose a topic. From there, whenever you add anything new, you can put a topic on it. You can do this with assignments as well that are already neatly put together as needed.

The classroom folder

If you're a teacher that isn't sure whether or not you've given a class an assignment, you can check the class folder. It's located right on the home page of where the classes are listed. You can check the class folder in the Google drive.

If you want to easily ensure that you have a good organization system for the students as well, you can simply make folders of all of the students at this point, and then throw the work into there each time it's put in. That way, you've got a great system, and one that works rightfully for you, no matter what the odds may be.

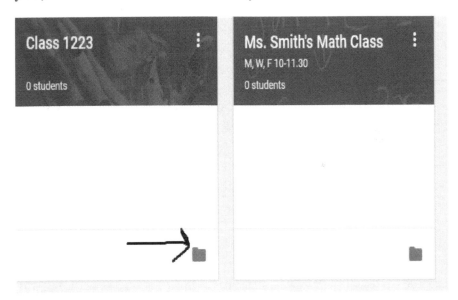

Commenting

Commenting is another big part, and it's mostly seen in the stream, or perhaps in a question that you assign. You can have two types, the class comments and the private comments. Class comments you see under every single post that's there, and you can see all of them usually just by clicking on it. With the assignment, as you see how many are done/not done, you'll be able to look at comments, and you as a teacher can provide comments as needed, simply by clicking the reply option under the student's comment.

first assignment due 8/20

Got it. Thanks| CANCEL   POST

Now, if needed, you should use private comments. These are those only seen by teachers, and they're available on assignments and questions. On the teacher side, you can go to student work, choose a student, and from there read a comment. You can then respond to it accordingly, based on what you need to say.

For students, you can go to any assignment, and at the bottom left corner, you can then add a private comment. The teacher can then get back to the student whenever possible, and give the help that they need.

For many teachers and students, knowing how to effectively create assignments is a great thing. It's so simple, since teachers can just make them in drive, submit them to the classroom, and then students can put the work in. If needed, the teacher can step in and give help, and announcements and posts are there to help the students improve their learning experience. With all of this put together, it's a simple, yet very effective, way to easily create the best classroom experience that you can, and do what you feel is right to help your students better understand Google Classroom.

5 Chapter – Inviting Students and Teachers to Classes

Let's say you have the whole classroom set up, and you've put together some great assignments for the year. But, what about inviting other students, teachers, and even parental guardians? Well, it's super simple, and this chapter will go over how you can invite both students and teachers to your classroom in order for this to work.

Having students join the classroom

One of the best ways to have students join this, is through a code, or by an email. A code is usually the easiest one, and requires a bit less work. Plus, if you don't have the emails of each student, it's a quick and easy way to get them to set up. Now, what you do, is you go to settings, and then choose the option to get the join code. You can then display the code to every single student, and then, they can log in with their Google account, press the plus button, choose to join the class, and then there you go, you now have students in your class. It's a much easier way, especially if you're someone that has a lot of students, and you typically don't have the contact information.

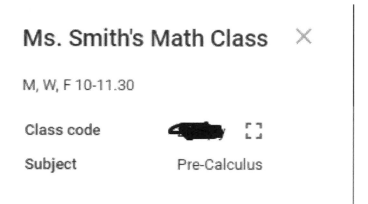

Ms. Smith's Math Class ✕

M, W, F 10-11.30

Class code

Subject   Pre-Calculus

If you've already got the students set up, and you want to set up a personal invite, you essentially begin by going to the people tab (used to be students) and from there, you choose the students that you'd like to invite here. If they're in a Google group already, they will be invited automatically. When you choose all of them, you then will send out emails to each of the students that you have, and they will then have to on their own end, choose the option to accept the invite, and then they are a part of this. Now, if you are using the G suite for education option, you can only add students that are in the Google domain, and if the students are using public email accounts, and not school email accounts, they won't be able to access the online content, and it was mostly put there to give extra security. However, it does add a bit of an extra step, so if you are in a district that doesn't have emails that are already readily available to students, usually the join code link is ultimately the better option.

Now, the email is ideally used when you have students that typically don't meet in person for classes, or maybe they do, but most of the focus is an online type of class. It's best if you make sure to encourage students to have an icon with their email address, as it does prevent the wrong person from getting the wrong contact information, and makes it easier on everybody at the end of the day. You can only do the Google group however, if you know the email addresses of every single student that's here.

Invite students

Type a name or email

CANCEL   INVITE

Adding Teachers to Google Classrooms

If you have a student teacher, or maybe a co-teacher that you collaborate with, having this extra little addition is pretty nice, since you can have consistency among each of the classes. With this, you can make sure that you have responsible, simple posting in each of the class. However, because Google classroom doesn't have the automatic option to add teachers, you need to make sure that you manually do so. That's because usually each class is viewed as an individual, but if you work together, you need to have both options. However, it's very easy to add a teacher to this class.

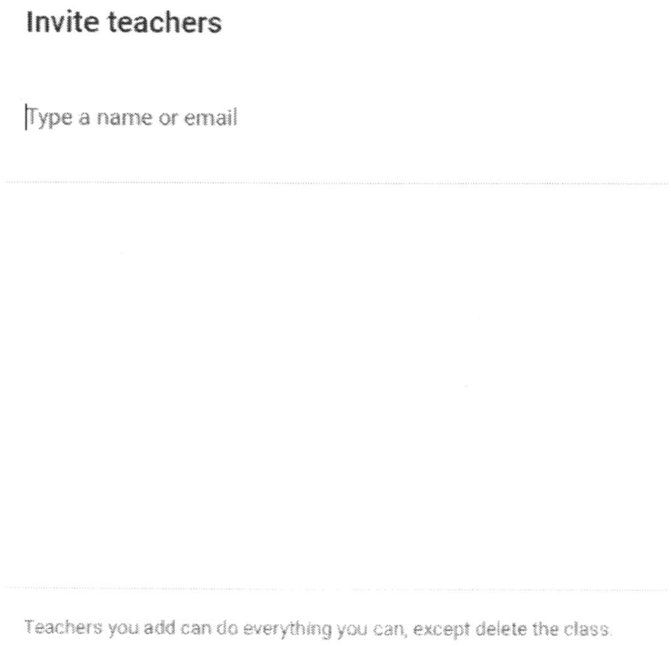

Invite teachers

Type a name or email

Teachers you add can do everything you can, except delete the class.

First, you go to the about tab, and choose the option to invite the teacher. From here, the teacher will need to accept the invite themselves, and then once they do, they will then be able to access the class and help the teacher with various aspects.

Adding Parents

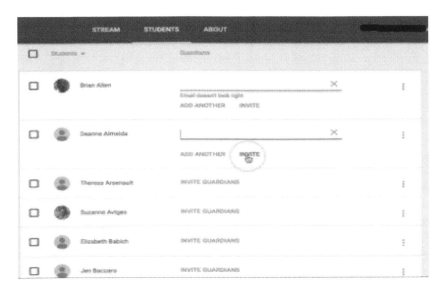

Adding parents and guardians is important in some cases, because it then allows the parent to be up-to-date on what is going on in the child's life and schooling. Parent notifications are also good because it informs them when something is due, and for parents who like to keep up with their child's activities, this is a big part of it.

For parents and guardians, they can be put into the notifications group. Essentially, you manage the notification by having the district admin allowing the email summaries in the settings, and once that's enabled, you go to your classroom, choose the guardian email notifications, and then you can include the class that's listed.

Now, what this does, is it'll give a learning management system to the parents. This is a bit of a newer update to the system, since before then, it involved needing a login with the domain to get in there, but nowadays, you essentially just add and then you go. The notifications are essentially summaries via email of what's going on with the student within the classes. These include work that's missing or late, any work that's coming up, and the activities within the class. What's more, is that the parents don't even need to log in, and it doesn't show the grades work or some other parts, which may limit, but that depends.

Now to invite parents, you go to students, and then, for each student, you can then invite the guardian, put in the email addresses, and then choose to invite, and you essentially, once they're connected, they have everything. Currently, you have to add each of the emails once at a time, and once the parents are given the email, you can accept, and then there they are. It's how you set this up. You can essentially as well, if you just want to email the guardians without the notifications, choose Google Classroom, then students, and then click ore next to each one, and then choose to email guardians. You can also use the option to email all guardians if possible.

For many teachers, adding parents, students, and other teachers helps to build a better network, and you can easily do all of this, and so much more, through the use of Google Classroom.

6 Chapter – How to Grade Assignments and then put Them on Google sheets

Then we have grading. Grading is a focal part of helping students understand and learn better, but it is a bit different with Google Classroom. Here, you'll learn all about how you can easily, and effectively, grade in Google Classroom, and how you can grade work within this.

To Begin with This

Now to begin, you essentially need the students to turn in the work, so you should wait for students to turn in their work, and then, once it's in, it's time for you to begin. You essentially log in, and you click the stream lab. You then can, if it isn't displayed already, you can check the assignments that are already there. You can check to see who is done, and not done. You can choose the one that's above done, and from there, you've got an expanded list on who has turned it in.

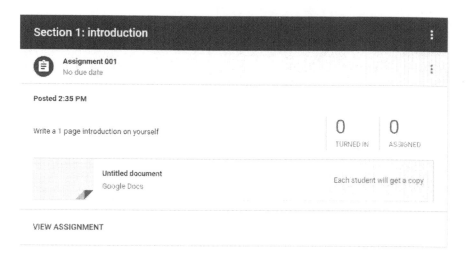

From there, you should then click on the name of the student themselves in order to see the assignment they have. From there, if they have an attachment to there, you essentially click the attachment, and then, you're given the appropriate Google app with the assignment that's on there.

At this point, you essentially will go into grading, and you can add comments and the like from there.

Commenting on Grades

At this point, you're then opening it up in drive. At this point too, you can start to comment. If you're a teacher who likes to grade with red pen for example, you can essentially go to the text button, change the color to red, and then comment. But, it's a bit easier this time around. If you want to, you can use the feature that allows you to comment to give the appropriate feedback. To do this, you highlight what you're about to comment, and then, choose the option to insert, and then comment. At that point, type in what you need, save it, and then, it's saved completely for the student. You can mark up the assignment as needed, or even leave positive comments if there is something that you should inform the student that they did well with.

At this point, you can from there, go to the classwork tab, then the assignment name, and then view it. If you haven't changed the value of the point system yet, you can always change it. From there, choose the student file that you've finished, and from there, enter the name, and then the grade. At this point, you return it to them for review.

There is that instance however, that if you want to change the grade itself, you can go to the assignment that the student has, and then enter the grade. You can also return these ungraded as needed too. Remember, that the changes to the grade only affect those not returned yet, and original ones have the same grade as before.

Returning Assignments to Students

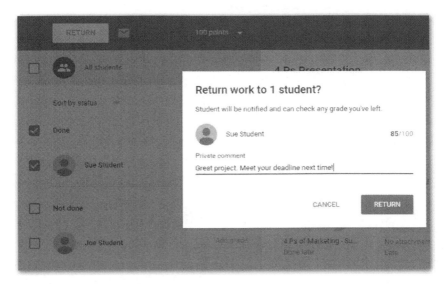

Assignments can be returned at this point to the student. You can then press the box that says return assignment. You then want to choose the option to return this, and you return this essentially before it's recorded. When it's recorded, it's essentially done with. That's up to you, and inevitably your choice. You can then press the option to return the assignment.

Now, if you have additional feedback, it'll give you an option to do that. Again, it's ultimately up to you. If you have no feedback, don't worry about this. If you do, then you should throw it in there before it's completely returned to the student. That's because, the student should know. Remember, it's better to be a bit overboard with grading if you have feedback that will help students become better, and to help them understand the subject at hand.

Tips on This

The first tip that we will say, is that when you're making assignments, don't use MS word. Instead, use the Google drive apps, since they are completely integrated with the classroom system. If you do use a Microsoft word file, it'll cause the student to have to download the files once more, upload these again, and then attach them. You also need to put in the extra work with downloading and reattaching, and it's just a lot of extra fluff that you don't need. Oh yes, the drive files are there for a reason, and they're super easy to create. Plus, if you export a sheet from MS word to drive, it works the same way, making it easy for everyone.

Another helpful tip, is that you can actually use shortcuts to add comments onto this. You can use control alt and then M to put comments into a document on Google docs. You can then press the enter key to close the comment, and then control plus W to actually close the document itself. You can also do feedback by choosing the name of the students, and then looking at the options to see what they've submitted. You can also go to the add private comment section on this, and you can also enter grades for students. You can't actually get a grade book with Google Classroom, just notify the grades though.

With Google Classroom as well, the key way to ensure that you're getting feedback to students quickly, is through adding the mobile app. It allows you to add comments to various projects, and answer questions on grades. Plus, it's integral if you want to make sure that a student. got the assignment or not.

Another Big and important tip, is to utilize the form templates to help with grades. The form template can be used to make a sheet with the names, and a checklist of various elements, including what they're missing, homework points, and other elements. By carrying this around, you can also grade the students, and it's good to have if you want to check out whether or not they have the homework done or not.

Another really cool thing, is that if you want to make your grading faster, use shorthand. Google docs knows immediately what you're saying, so if you use short hand, and you type in the letters "wc" it will automatically change this to word choice, which will communicate to the students that it's bad word choice. It makes your life so much easier, especially if you're going through grading multiple papers.

It's also important for teachers to remember, that if you give an assignment back, the teacher can't edit it anymore. That means that if you have to edit anything else, they need to submit it to you again. You can notify them, and they can look at it, and if they resubmit it with changes, and you edit it and it's all good, you can also edit the grades by looking at the grade, pressing it, and then choosing the option to update the grade.

Exporting Grades

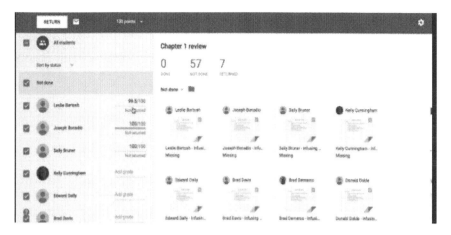

Finally, let's talk about exporting grades. Grades can be exported, and they're used to make sure that you have a place for all of them. Remember, this just displays the grades, and isn't' a biodegrade, but if you want to help export these so that they're all written down, you can do this. Lots of teachers like to export these into a .csv file, or through Google sheets. You can with sheets, create an average for the class, and for students, and along with this, you can actually set up arrows from a grade box to another one, which makes it faster.

To export these grades into sheets, you essentially go to Google Classroom, choose your class, and then the assignments. From here, you go to settings, and choose the option to copy all of the grades into Google sheets. From there, an automatic spreadsheet is created on the drive folder, allowing you to see all the grades. Currently though, you can only export these on the desktop version of classroom, not on mobile version or via the app.

Copy all grades to Google Sheets

Download all grades as CSV

Download these grades as CSV

Now, to export these grades to a CSV file, you'll be able to have all of the grades in one place. This is good for if you're trying to keep every single grade in one place, and if you want to print these out. To do this, you essentially go to Google Classroom again, click on the class you want to choose, and then, go to settings once again, and choose an option, whether to either download the assignment grades for that one only, or to download all of the assignment and question grades. For the first, you choose to download these grades as a CSV, and for the assignment and question grades, you choose to download all grades as a CSV. From there, you can find them in your downloads folder, and you can bring them up on your word processing device accordingly.

For many teachers, the element of grading is made so much easier with Google Classroom. With this, you can easily create the environment that you want to create, and from there, you've got it all set up so that students can access this easily. It's easy, and simple to achieve, so you'll be able to create the best and easiest classroom experience that they can possibly have.

7 Chapter – How to Motivate Pupils

As a teacher, sometimes you need some good ways to motivate pupils. Here are a few ways that you can help motivate students in an online classroom learning environment.

Front Row math Program

This is a program that was begun by a startup company, and it makes math fun. It involves providing various activities and games for students in grades K-8, and each time this is done, the teachers get progress reports. This is used to help with kids who are struggling early with math, and also to help them not just copy from the books.

Front Row works to change this, creating a tailor-made plan for children so that they can understand math better. It's used today by more than 25,000 different elementary and middle school kids, and you can get either a free or paid version. With this, teachers get reports on how students do, and they can help if they do have trouble. It helps to give a personalized idea on how to better understand math.

With this app, you're essentially letting students work on both math, English, Science, and social studies lessons, since front row is actually a subset of the Freckle Education app. They're given little games based on different concepts, and each student can work at their own pace. Teachers can step in as needed, and help students whenever there is trouble. The games are actually fun, and not just the same blackboard math texts that you may see in a traditional classroom. By making it individualized, you can help those who have fallen behind, and help those who get it to continue on forward without making anyone else feel bad.

Google Classroom Book Club

This is something that you as a teacher will need to set up, but it's a great way for you to get students to read. A book club helps inspire students to read more. How you can do it, is put together a book club with a code, and from there, set up small challenges. For example, you can have them take pictures of a book that they recently read, and say why it's a good read. They can do this with every book they read, and maybe they get a star, and after a certain amount, they get a prize that they like. You can even take this to the next level, such as in the case of having students post about it, giving their recommendations, and for extra points, they can have other students respond, and tell you why they liked or didn't like this book. You can keep them going. You can even give incentive by saying you can get extra points for discussing this n class, telling them about this book. It's a bit of a more hands-on program that you will need to put together, but if you want to motivate a student, sometimes adding in a book club can make a difference.

Encourage Self-Monitoring

This is another element of Google Classroom that you can keep in mind. Lots of times, students like to be self-motivated, and you need to make sure that you do give students a chance to look at their progress. For example, implementing backboard on there can help students improve on this, and they can look at the discussions, projects, assignments and the like, and you can with Google Classroom as well, have them focus on their own personal progress to make it so that they're curious about the progress that they make. Putting together discussion forums on Google Classroom, having students see their grades, are surefire ways to help them get motivated with education in a rightful manner.

Acknowledge the Challenges

When you're trying to get students excited to work on a subject, you should give them a challenge. Once a week, give them a challenge, may e make it extra credit or something. From there, you can essentially use this in order to get students interested in working harder. If you acknowledge that it's a challenge, and encourage students to find the answer, and with the right incentive, you should make sure that you tell them they can do it.

Videos Help

One thing that you should consider, especially if you're a teacher in a class that doesn't meet a lot, is to make a message for students to see, whether it be a text, or even a video message, and throw it on the home page. You as a teacher can get a lot of great results from this, since students will see that the teacher is involved, and that a big part of some student's ability to actually work with a class, and get the results that they want from it. Being involved is a two-way street, and as a teacher, you should always get students working together.

Scratch

Want to get your student's creative juices going, all while creating a healthy online learning environment.? Scratch is a way to do it. This is an MIT site that allows students to make various projects online, and you can export these to others. This is great if you're a teacher that wants to help teach students about symmetry and other concepts, and from there, show it to other students. This is a way to get students to be creative, and you can connect this with Google Classroom, have them work with it, and from there, you can also get them to show it to the teacher for extra credit.

Extra Credit!

With all of these, the best thing to add to this, is of course, extra credit. By building these activities, you'll be able to motivate students to do them. Lots of students want to make sure that their grade is intact, and sometimes, the best way to ensure that it is, is through extra credit. While some students may prefer to just not do these, if grades are in jeopardy, it'll get them to start using these activities, and it's a way to encourage students to use the tools as well.

By making sure you to motivate students, you'll get them excited to learn, which in turn will help them feel more excited about learning, and bettering themselves. If you know how to motivate them, they will do well, and you as a teacher will have a much easier time with your class too.

8 Chapter – The Best Google Classroom extensions

Extensions are great ways to help improve your ability to use Google Classroom. It makes your experience even better, and this chapter will go over the top ones that you should have in your arsenal, and for students in teachers, this makes it better.

Send by Gmail

If you want to show off shareable content that you feel is relevant, whether it be for the classroom discussion, or maybe you need this for research, there is an extension that you can use now. By adding send from Gmail, you'll be able to share with others the content, and it can make actually sending various elements including documents and articles, much easier for you.

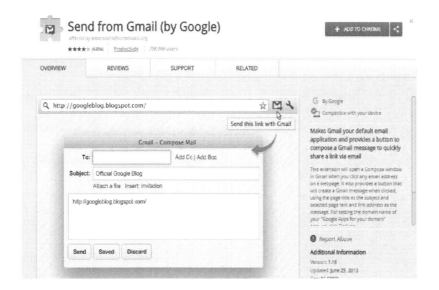

Share to classroom

This is an extension made for teachers who want to share web pages to the entire classroom, instantly happening on all student's computers. This is good for if you're teaching a lesson, and you want to show it to every student. This helps, since they won't have to sift through and try to find the web page, and it'll keep them on the right track. This is also used for announcements, assignments, and various web pages you want to share. You can share this with all the students instantly, but make sure that you have it active on all of the devices. Students can also do this back to teachers too, which is pretty cool. Students can only share this to the teacher though, not everyone, and you can mute notifications on this if you don't want to have it all over your device.

Power Thesaurus

For many students, power thesaurus is a way for students to look up various antonyms, along with synonyms for anything that they want to desire. You essentially, when you have this on there, you can double click this word from the icon on the toolbar, and then, you can show off what the word means, and any similar, or dissimilar words. This is perfect if you as a student, or even a teacher, want to beef up your own personal vocabulary.

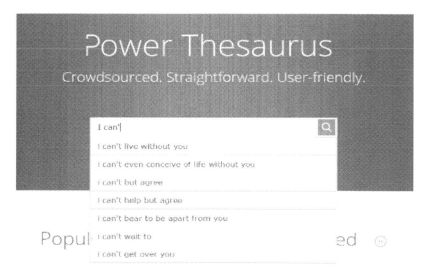

Save to Google Drive

this is a great way for students who are doing research projects to save all of their content to a Google drive. This saves so much time, especially if you're already working in the other Google tools as well. By enabling this, you essentially can save anything that you want, whether it be screenshots, pictures, or even web content, and throw that directly onto the drive itself, to make your life all the more easier. It can change your productivity, and pairing it with the other tools can miraculously change this.

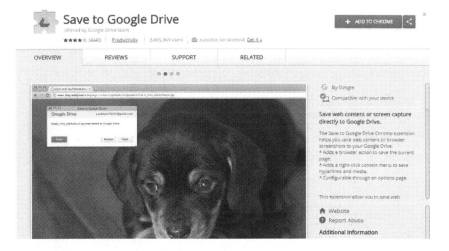

LastPass

One thing that can be frustrating, for both students and teachers, especially if there are educational software that they use, is the amount of passwords that you have to remember. It can be quite annoying, but with LastPass, you'll be able to manage all of your passwords, and have them saved. Of course, this does have a couple of privacy concerns, but it does work if you're someone who is just sick of trying to remember a million different passwords, and wants it all managed in a simplified manner.

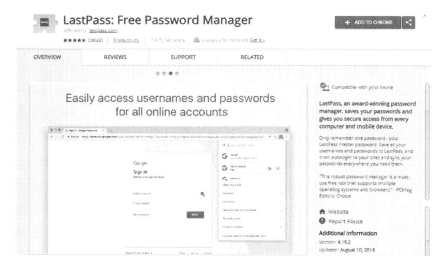

LastPass: Free Password Manager

Google URL Shortener

This is good for teachers that want to share many websites. If you're talking to students, and you want to link something to them, it can be a bit distracting. This also is a bit annoying if you're a teacher who likes to add links, but they're lines long. With the goo.gl URL shortener, you'll be able to shorten any URL with just clicking it. You can also make some QR codes to send to other students and teachers, and if you're using handouts and want to share the URL, you can do so easily with this. It's quite nice, and makes your life simpler.

G Suite Training

this is a free extension that works wonders for teachers and students, and if you have any question on how to use this software, this is ultimately the way for you to go. You can get tutorial videos, interactive training, and even customer support help if you need it. what's more, if you're a student who has issues, don't think this is limited to just teachers, because students can learn through these videos too how to navigate through the Google Classroom software, and from there, be able to accomplish all the tasks that they have on hand. It's quite simple.

Read&Write

This is a great extension if you're casting your screen, and you want it to read it out loud. This is also good for students who want to multitask various articles, and hear what's being read. This is a great extension that essentially reads out loud what is on there. This is good for those who are ESL, or are dyslexic too, since it allows them to better understand what they're reading, and it also can be used to help check grammar too. It's like digital proof reading for students so that their content sounds good, or if you want to read something but don't feel like staring at a screen, this is the extension that will help you.

Grammarly

If you're a student, or a teacher, who wants to make sure they have their grammar and spelling correct, this is the way to do it. It's a great way to have a second set of eyes on everything, and this is a free chrome extension. Essentially, it revises anything that's typed in, and allows you to have correction suggestions to make it easier. While it may not always be correct, it allows you to have explanations that give you good options for you to try. It's a great extension to help with student and teacher learning.

Adblock

Ads are annoying. AdBlock is one of those extensions that

you should always have. You can get just general AdBlock, but there is also AdBlock for YouTube, which allows you to literally block all the ads that come from YouTube, which allows you to browse this without getting distractive content. Have you ever wanted to showcase a video, only to find out that it's got ads all over the place that are utterly annoying? Well, now you can eliminate this with this extension, and with just downloading this, all of those annoying ads are gone.

Emoji for Chrome

This is a good one if you're going to send lots of messages to other students. Emojis are good to communicate sometimes, even with just an acknowledgment. It's easy if you want to have a way to find, use, and copy different emojis, and it's a good way to communicate with others on the web. After all, a good emoji might be just the right way to communicate to other people various needs, or even how to respond to various assignments. A thumbs up can be a good acknowledgment; you know?

These extensions will change your ability to use Google Classroom, and for both students and teachers alike, it's a great way to really ensure that you have the best results from this, and to help make your classroom experience better.

9 Chapter – Top Five Hidden Features of Google Classroom

Did you know that there are some hidden features within Google Classroom that can change the experience? This chapter will go over the top 5, why they matter, and how you can use them to better your experience.

Templates

If you're a teacher, this is actually a good feature to remember. While it may not be a "hidden" feature, it's often completely overlooked. If you're looking for a good template to show off notes, a letter, or even formalize any document, then this is something that you should consider. This is also good for students, especially if they tend to have class projects that they need to remember to finish. For example, if they are to write a mock resume, it is much easier to do it with this template, than just a generic document that you can make in Google docs. This is a great feature, and you can find that on the homepage of the Google doc, and there are so many that by pressing the more button, you can look at all of the options.

The Hidden Assignment Calendar

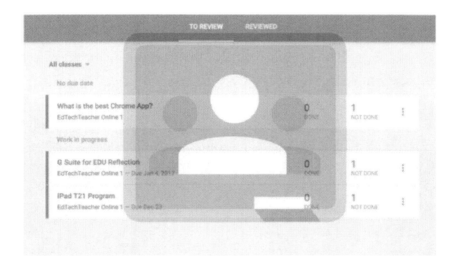

This is an assignment calendar that's used to keep both students and teachers working together. Every time teachers create questions, there's due dates attached to it, and you can see this immediately on the calendar of Google classroom. To find this, you want to go to the menu lines, and once you do, you want to press the area that says calendar. Once that's shown, you can see right then and there any of the work that's assigned to your class, and anything that's due soon. Teachers also get the G suite calendar, which can be used to put assignments in too, and you can access it directly to add different events that they have. For example, field trips, tutoring, or even meetings can be put on there. You can also add general school events too so that every single student is on the right track with this, in order to help keep everyone together.

Research Tool

This is a tool for those in Google docs that want to have some online research added to their projects. It's actually super simple, since it allows for you to refer to images and research without leaving the document, which means that you don't have to click so many different tabs. It's an underrated, and often overlooked tool, but it's been there, you just probably never knew about it. You can either open it from the tools section, right click a word to research, or you can press control, alt, shift, and then I. You then are given a whole bunch of topics related to what you put in there, whether it be general Wikipedia articles, images, scholarly articles on this, and then you can choose the content, and put it in there, and you can also cite this easily. It's an underrated tool that's actually a godsend for many people who do research papers, since it allows you to use all of this right away, and makes your learning experience easier. It's a hidden feature of Google Classroom, and it allows for the experience to be even better for the students and teachers.

Copy Header

If you're making a Google sites page, such as a student website, this is actually a great tool that can be used to help improve the navigation of this site. Every time you create a new page, you're given a header that's blank, but some teachers want to use a similar heading, or even the same one for every single page that they have. If you want to do this, the first thing you do is you want to click the page that has the banner to reuse. From there, you'll press the icon with a plus on there, and then choose the option to add to new page, and that basically causes it to be copied over once again. It's a hidden feature for teachers who are employing Google sites within their Google Classroom software, and it can make a difference. If you want to save a little bit of time, and can make your life easier.

Filtering searches

This is a hiding place that's in plain sight. At the very top of the drive, you'll see an arrow that goes down, along the edge of this. From there, once you click on it, you'll be given many different search options, or to filter different search results. This is kind of a lifesaver for teachers, because if you've got a ton of different projects that are happening down the pipeline, you really want to have a way to make it so that you're able to get all of these files. If you have a large library period as a student, this is a great way to narrow down the results. as well. You can filter this by the different file types, the names of each of the files, and even the date it's been modified by the person as well. For those documents that are shared, you can filter it by the people you've shared the file too. You can also with this utilize the action item that comes with this, or any suggestions you'd like to do to the file. It's a good way to help you with organizing your drive, and you'll notice that, for both students and teachers who use Google Classroom, it saves you a lot of time. After all, if you're a teacher who teaches multiple sections, or covers a lot of course content, it can be a nightmare to keep up with all of this, but this will make your life all the more easier in the long run.

These features are in some cases hidden in plain sight, but a lot of them are underrated tools that can facilitate your experience. For the average teacher or student, these various features can make a world of a difference in your ability to use this, so it's definitely important to make sure that you use these different actions, and different features, since it can help you with improving your life.

10 Chapter – Top Five Hidden Features of Google Classroom

Do you want some great apps for learning? This chapter will go over a couple of apps that can change your experience with Google Classroom. Read on to find out more.

Math Apps

Here are some math apps that should be included to better your experience:

The first is Motion Math. This is an innovative tool that teaches foundations for math, with some interactive visuals. With this, you can integrate it into your lesson plan. Students can do these problems at the pace that they like, and you as a teacher just have to make sure that you have them doing it. It is good for grades K-6, and it can give instructions on how to solve problems with context, and it does measure the learning of students with a growth mindset, and allows for visuals to be used to understand math.

Quick Math Pack is a bundle of four different apps that allow for some quick learning opportunities for a student. These are for grades K-5 as well, and it goes over basic math concepts, fractions, and also telling time. For four bucks, you can have this app bundle, and they're great for students who want some extra practice with learning various math concepts. It also comes with a handwriting software, allowing the student. To write it onto the interface to better remember math concepts.

Apollonius is a geometry app for students who want to learn basic geometry. It's used to help showcase various constructions that are made, and it can be made with both a compass and a ruler, using this to explore the different kinds of objects that you can make. It is used with touchscreen devices, so that you can get the best experience that you can with this app. It's good for learning basic shapes too, and for some, it can help you better understand how angles and lines interact with one another.

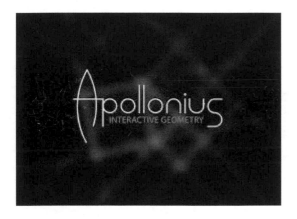

Mathspace is a computer-based math system that allows students to have problems fully worked out, and get instant feedback and help. It contains over 70,000 different questions, ranging from algebra, graphing, geometry, statistics, and geometry. You can use this for students anywhere from grades 6-12, meaning that it's a great app for those older students. It's also got math writing recognizing software, where it will recognize the items that are written, and correct them on the spot, giving you hands-on help for bettering your understanding of difficult concepts. This is usually where students tend to fall behind in math, and this software can prevent that from happening accordingly.

Assorted VR Apps

VR is super popular these days, to the point where Google Classroom has a couple apps on it itself. But, here are the best apps to use relating to VR.

Animal flashcards is a great way to use AR with flashcards, allowing children to learn about various animals and also learn the letters easier. It's a unique app, and you get realistic rendered animals to look at. You can tap the image to hear the name, and the letters that are in the name of the animal.

Quiver is coloring but made for learning. It's AR coloring, which means that you can color some interesting characters with this technology, view cool animals, play interactive games, and even get quizzes and facts on it. You can learn about many different animals and other factors with this fun app, and it certainly allows you to explore your own personal artistic side as well.

Quiver

Boulevard is an art teacher's dream. With this, you essentially get the VR and AR experience of going to different museums, to look at the works that are there. Sure, you may not be able to take your class to the British museum, but this app allows you to explore this experience, and if you're an art teacher who wants to work on art history, or even a history teacher that dabbles in art, this is for you.

Skill Building Apps

This section will go over apps that are good to just build skills with, whether generalized learning, or other skills that come from this.

Khan academy is one that allows you to get video explanations on anything, from math, economics, history, and more, and it comes with interactive practices, related to common core, and other learning tools that allow you to help improve with learning, and you can flex your muscles by understanding different concepts. It's also set to help with standardized tests too, which makes it even better, and a very good app for general skill building.

SentenceBuilder is a great app for those who want to get better at building and creating sentences. For those who want to get better at grammar, this is for you. With this, it will allow children in elementary school to build sentences and concepts, and it mostly focuses on bettering ones understanding of connecting words, which is a focal part and a problem that many who try to understand the English language. There are pictures to make sentences with, and it does use reinforcement to correct this, and teachers can even track the progress of students as well.

For students who need a bit of help organizing their lives and homework, Studious is the answer for this. It's a homework planner that allows students to organize and improve their ability to keep track of everything. you'll get reminders of when assignments are due, when tests are coming up, and you can even take notes and send emails. It is great, because you can scan and print documents from your phone, create a personal assignment calendar, organize your assignments to be prepared, and allow you to edit your courses and such, giving you a chance to improve your ability to understand classes.

American wordspeller is great for those who want to better their own understanding of words, learn how to spell them correctly, and allows you to type it in how it sounds to you. It's a way to understand how some words are spelled, and it can help you to better understand the English language. English can be hard, since there are so many different words out there, but this can help you understand the word meaning, and help to prevent you from getting confused about certain words that are out there, such as how carrot/karat/carat all sound the same.

Stack the countries is a great app to help you learn where countries are, and it's good if you're in a geography or social studies class. In this, you literally get a map, with some animated little countries, and from there, you literally drop them wherever you want. You want to build and stack all of these countries correctly to help you win levels. It allows you to better understand the locations of different places, and you can even choose to focus on a continent, or even the entire world, and it even comes with flash cards to help you brush up on your geography as well.

Finally, we've got Evernote. It essentially is a great app for organizing your notes, and your life. You can hand write notes on a device, save them, and then organize them. For those who don't like to use the handouts, or like to take their own notes and the teacher doesn't provide notes, this is great. Plus, it allows you to have a better understanding of all your notes, in order to make your learning experience so much better.

With all of these apps, you'll see here that Google classroom can work with many different apps to make it better. While yes, some are paid, others are free, and you as a student, or even as a teacher, can benefit from all of these. Using these can make your experience worthwhile, and can help you become a better learner.

11 Chapter – Google Classroom Vs. Apple classroom

Finally, let's talk about Google Classroom versus Apple classroom. Google Classroom is the focus of this book, but how does it stack up to Apple classroom? Well, read on to find out. This chapter will discuss the Google Classroom features, and how it stacks up to the other competitor.

The Hardware difference

The biggest difference that you'll run into is the hardware elements. Apple classroom is free for iPad, and essentially, the classroom involves using multiple different iPad, and the teachers will put these on the device, allowing students to use these as an integrative tool. The teacher iPad is essentially a collection of these powers, in order to give a learning experience. Essentially, it's similar to Google Classroom, and once this is configured, it's connected to devices, and the iPad are shared, and once the session is done, it can be signed out of. It's a way to keep students focused, shows students different screens, and it can share documents with the class through the use of AirDrop. It also shows student work on Apple TV, reset the passwords for students, and it also can create groups of students based on the apps that they use, and it allows teachers to create groups and teams. Basically, it's a way to have Apple within the classroom, and through the use of the iPad, it's more collaborative directly within the direct learning atmosphere.

Good for lower Level Grades

Now, you'll notice immediately, that the only similarity is that they both have the word "classroom" in there. This means, that Apple classroom is more of a direct classroom tool, and it helps teachers show apps and pages to students that might have trouble with this, and show off the work that's there. Teachers in upper grades benefit from this because it monitors the activity, but the thing is, the student can find out if the teacher is watching very fast. It's more of a direct device to use for learning within the classroom, whereas with Google Classroom, it focuses on both in and outside of the classroom.

Google Classroom focuses on organization

One big part of Google Classroom, is the organization element. It is all collaborated with Google drive, which essentially means that learning based on connections and education is there based on organization than directly into the classroom. Google Classroom makes it easy for teachers to assign the work, and allows students to have better organization on assignments and allows them to get updates faster. It also allows it to go paperless too, which is a big plus. Google Classroom focuses on showing work that needs to be done, any grades that they have, and any assignments that they missed. It's more of a tool to better organization of the student body over everything else.

Apple Classroom Has more interactive Lessons

For those teachers that want to have a more engaging class, and that's where Apple Classroom may work better. For example, if you're teaching a younger crowd, it may be better to have Apple classroom, because let's face it, do first graders really need to navigate Google drive and submit documents? Course not. They would benefit more from Apple classroom, since it involves showing the app, and allows teachers to teach, and students to focus on what the teacher is teaching. It's focused as well on interacting with the student, and it shows the assignment that they work on, giving teachers a chance to look at each of the pieces of work that the student does, and the most recently used options. There even the screen view that shows the iPad, and it is a good way to keep direct focus on the students within the classroom.

So if you're a more interactive-lesson focused teacher, such as you're teaching students the colors, or want students to not screw around in class, the Apple Classroom device may be a better option for you. If you're a teacher who is more interested in having essays, homework, and other elements easily organized in one place, then yes, Google Classroom may be more your style.

Google Classroom allows for Multiple Devices to Be Used

now, you can get the tablets for Google Classroom, but if you want to have students work on something right away, they totally can. The beauty of Google Classroom, is that it's not attached to a brand. You can get Google on your computers, and installing chrome is super easy. With that, you are given way more options on using this. Google Classroom can be downloaded as an app too on our device, meaning that if you've got a phone, tablet, or whatever, you're essentially free to use this with whatever you want. That's what's so nice about it, because students can work on assignments right away, and from there, submit it to the teacher. It also allows for students to work on different subjects while on the go, and can share different questions and resources with the teacher. It is much more interactive, and is perfect for if you have a classroom with multiple smart devices.

The problem with Apple, is that it's a brand. you're essentially working only with Apple brand, meaning that it's highly limited. After all, not everyone may have a Mac, or an iPad, so it doesn't really have as much use as say Google Classroom does.

You don't Have to Choose

The reality of this though, is that there are some key differences, and you can choose based on needs, with Apple classroom being more of a focus directly within the class environment itself, and Google classroom being more on workflow and assignments. They're two different tools, but comparing it is like Apples and oranges, which is a bit different from your average device comparison, since it's often pitted against each other in the technology realm. The truth is, you shouldn't have to choose between both of them, because some teachers benefit from both. If you really want to make your classroom the best it can be, sometimes the best answer is to add both of these services, since they're both really good at what they do, and they complement each other well. The answer is, you shouldn't choose one or the other. If you want to get both, get both. If the district can handle both, get both. But, if you're a teacher for a younger group of students, Apple classroom works. If you're a teacher for older students, Google Classroom works.

Apple classroom and Google Classroom are two very different types of software, but both of them accomplish the goal of helping children learn better, so that they can use these skills to better their life now, and in their future learning endeavors and studies that they will embark on

Conclusion

For many teachers, they've taken the first step to changing how they run the classroom with Google Classroom. It's a platform that can be used to help teachers and students alike benefit from this activity. With Google Classroom, you get the extra benefit of being able to really help plan your classrooms effectively, and get them into the spirit of taking their education to new heights. Teachers love this system, because it keeps everything in one place, and with the advent of virtual classrooms, and having everything on the computer, it's only made learning easier.

Google is coming out with new and improved learning tools as well, such as the tablets that you can get for your students, which help them keep learning. With these additions, along with Google Classroom, your ability to teach the students core curriculum that they need in order to be successful is totally possible, and worth it.

With that being said, let's discuss the next step that you as an educator, parent, guardian, or student should take in order to get the most out of this. For teachers, start to plan your lessons based off this system, and put together the plan and such. You can from there, for the parents and students, get into this, and you can all keep up with the child's education. Many parents have trouble taking the initiative, but if you have it all together, you'll be able to create the perfect scholarly plan for your pupils, and everyone can learn what they want to learn with this amazing system. Learning is being taken to a new, digital future, and Google Classroom is providing that, and so much more.

Thanks for buying the book!

I hope you liked reading my book.

P

DATE DUE

PRINTED IN U.S.A.

Made in the USA
Middletown, DE
08 March 2019